WANDERINGS

WANDERINGS

POETRY FROM THE DREAMER

NIHAR SHARMA

www.facebook.com/thedreamerdiary

www.instagram.com/thedream_diary

www.twitter.com/thedream_diary

ISBN: 0-9983811-0-1

ISBN-13: 978-0-9983811-0-7

This book is a work of fiction. Names, characters, places, and
incidents either are products of the author's imagination or are
used fictitiously. Any resemblance to actual events or locales or
persons, living or dead, is entirely coincidental.

Cover illustration by Katarzyna Surman.

Dedicated to Reality
for annoying me enough
that I was compelled to daydream.

#1

And I have dreamt of you,
the way the deserts dream of the rain
and the mountains dream of the sea shore,
the way the dead dream of living, and all
mortals dream of salvation.
I have dreamt of you,
the way all mere things dream of reaching
the unattainable. And when I find you,
for I surely will, I shall tell you
that I have dreamt of you,
that some dreams do come true, and maybe,

mine breathed you to life.

#2

She twisted and twirled
in the grass
to a music
that only she could hear.

They saw her and whispered
'she must be mad'

for who would want
 to dance
in the sun,
 under the wide
blue sky,
 with the wind
in their hair,
 the scent of
heaven
 and
the taste
 of freedom?

'Who would want that?'
they asked
and
 whispered

'she
must
be
mad.'

#3

I want to hold your hand
but
I'm scared
of what comes
 after,
scared that you may
come too close,
and see the screwed up
 failure
that I am,
the black pools of misery
that lie
 within me,
and all the dark corners
where I hide.

I don't know
what love is.
people glorify it too much.
All I know is,

I want to
hold
your
hand.

#4

He watched her
from the coffee house
as she walked
towards the book store
every morning.
Then
he would take out
a battered photo album,
look at their old pictures
and trace her features
with his thumb.
But
he couldn't go back
for it was over
and 'it's over'
has rules.

She watched his old Harley
parked outside
the coffee shop
as she went to work
every morning.
There
she would open
her worn out diary
and write about him,
all that he was,
and all that he had been.
But
she couldn't go back
for it was over
and 'it's over'
has rules.

It is
ironic,
that
the ones
who strive
for love
are considered
weak
while those
who advocate
war
are called
strong.

For
it takes
immense
strength
to commit to
and
bear the pain
of love
whereas
the weak
always find
a way
 to blame
someone else.

He courts chaos,
finds no beauty in order,
no gleam in perfection.
It is the free spirits,
the fields of wildflowers,
the moss covered walls,
the unmetalled tracks,
that sing to him.

Her parents treated her
as a figurine
of delicate bone,
a suffocated flower,
always sheltered
beneath stone.

But they didn't realize

that the stones
had lit a spark,
the bones drank in
the flames,
and the dried petals
fell away

to
reveal
a soul
that was on

fire.

He loved
and protected her,
but not in the
enclosing,
suffocating way

not like the wall
which keeps
a flower
in its persistent shadow,
for the flower
will wilt,
but like the wall
on which
a vine
finds support,
and slowly rises,
never held back,
until it
 grows
and spreads
into every inch,
every corner

of him.

She watched him
smoking in a corner
and for
a tiny, fleeting moment
she wanted to be
 that cigarette
to ignite to life
in his hands
tenderly
touch his lips
and then
 burn to ash
slowly,
intimately,
killing him
in the process.

They would both
be immortalized

for it was
the greatest triumph
over death
to die
 in the arms
of the one you love.

The stars twinkled
in his eyes,
and the Sun itself
warmed his smile.

I knew I might burn.

But
I just
had
to inch
a
little

closer.

#11

I think
I was meant
to be around people
and yet not be around them
to observe them from
a distance
and
wonder what
their
stories
are.

When she cried
the tears fell down
and buried themselves
 deep
within the earth,
only to sprout back
into a garden
of roses.
And sometimes,
towards dawn
and near dusk,
you could find
each flower
 still weeping
in her pain.

His eyes reflect
the dull grey
of a cloudy night,
still
and listless,
yet, on a few,
rare occasions
a breeze
blows
strong enough to
stir them
and
give you a glimpse of
 the stars
still burning within.

#14

I'm running away

not because
I hate you
or I don't want you.

I'm running away
because
you're too good
for me
and this
despicable person
that I am,
I never learnt to love.

My soul lurks
in crevices
where even I
have failed to reach.
And I'm so afraid
that if you entrust yours
in my keep
I'll carelessly
 let it fall.

And I'm so scared
that when I
finally find mine
it won't be as
bright as yours.
It'll be stained
and broken
and you will not want to stay.

And so
I'm running away.

#15

They say
'home is
where
the heart is'

and hers was
in the dusty
old bookshelves
in a run down
library
at the corner
and a broken,
withered
dance stage
where she had once
performed
with honour.

In these fading
 memories
her heart would often roam
lost in a world
forgotten
she yearned to go home.

#16

She was like glistening water
vibrant and full of life
and he was the parched earth
wondering if it was just
another mirage
he had stumbled upon.

And one day, he finally decided to show her his soul.
Yet she saw something in the shape of a hideous uneven rock
and she trembled, wanting to leave, but he called out
to her, gesturing to come closer. As she stepped towards
him, she realized that the broken, ragged edges were,
in essence, deep carvings that others had left upon him.
He encouraged her to carve something of her own, something
that was precious to her spirit, and as she closed her eyes
to search within, it occurred to her, how beautiful it was
to be able to be herself, without pretence, even if for
a little while. Thus, she carved, knowing that it was a
fragment of her own soul which she was engraving into his,
and smiled in the solace that even if she lost herself
someday, there would, at least, be one place where a piece
of her would always remain, accepted in its true form.

I'm not really sure of what I seek.
There are bits of you that cling to
me and talk to me in my solitude,
pieces that I remember as though it
was yesterday. But some fragments
have flown away, missing parts from
the jigsaw and although they are
yours, but somehow they are mine.
I don't think I miss you.
I miss me.
And sometimes I try to put it
together when people ask me who I am.
I fill up the vacant spaces with
untruths and fairy tales.
It's easy to spin up stories,
the tough part is hoping
that maybe, just maybe,
one person,
will read between the lines.

#19

She touched her broken wings
and wondered
if she had ever flown
or had it been a fading echo
of a dream long gone?

His eyes follow her through a packed street in the big
city, as she crosses the road and daintily springs on
to the sidewalk. She walks in a weird way, slightly
jumping with every step, as though gravity has less of
a hold on her, keeping one foot exactly in front of the
other, like a balancing act on a tightrope, so as not to
overstep a coloured piece of parallel strip painted on the
pavement. Some people give her a passing glance, an amused
smile here, a frown there, yet she continues to walk that
way, oblivious to everyone around her, including the simple
fact, that in a crowd of hunched shoulders and lowered necks,
to him she looks like a young flower, which has succeeded
in breaking through the concrete and now stands out alone,
among the stones, with a brilliant, untouched, unfathomed,
radiance.

#21

He was like
the morning sun
sometimes streaming
through the
window to my soul
illuminating
bits of broken pieces
which, at first,
would cower away
from the
intense glare
being kept in the dark
for too long
but then
would slowly peek out
wanting to feel
the warmth
again
    and again
        and again.

You're
 gone

and I am just
staring
at the clock
 wondering
who made
the damn thing
and why
do the seconds
tick by
even though
for me
 time
has stopped
and
growth
has stopped.
The blood
doesn't rush through
my veins
and I do not feel
the pillow
where I lie
for everything
is cold
and I can't
fall asleep
and I
can't
breathe.

Her broken pieces lay scattered across the floor.
He slowly lifted one. The sharp edges stung him,
cutting into his skin and making him bleed, but,
he hid the hurt somewhere behind his smile, and
continued to pick the others up. She watched him
in disbelief, wary with distrust, not understanding
why someone was making the effort to put her
together, when nobody had ever done so before.
People came, tried to pick up a shattered portion,
but withdrew as soon as it pinched them. Then why
was he still here? His hands were now a shade of
red, covered in cuts and bruises, a reflection of
her heart. Slowly, carefully, he helped rebuild
her, yet she was not herself anymore, for each
piece had been marked with his fingerprints and
smeared with his blood. The black of her sorrows
was fading away, yet she was now coloured in a
sweeter pain.

#24

Try as I may
I cannot shake off this feeling
of fear
of losing every little joy
which is finding its way
to me,
and so I tend to not let myself
accept to be happy.
But then I wonder,
do we hide from the day
in fear that we may not adjust
to the dark of the night?
I realize, sometimes I do,
I hide in a corner
to not let the sun rays touch my skin,
yet somehow
the warmth still finds a means to reach me
and I guess,
it is the same case with happiness.

25

As he crossed the street
their eyes met
for a fraction of a second
he would never forget
but before his breath returned
suddenly, she was gone
he forgot his errand
and found his way home

trying to put a name
to the emotion
burning his soul raw
his trembling fingers
pulled out the old pencils
and he began to draw

but no matter how much he tried
it would not come right
the fierceness in her eyes
would set the paper on fire
the curve of her lips
would dissolve the thin leaf
the wisp of hair around her neck
would not come close to desire

for beauty like that
could not be frozen
the iridescent colours
of a spirit so free
yearn he did, to share it
with the world
yet it had only been meant
for his eyes to see.

When people
lose
the will to live,
 whom
do I
condemn?
For
have they
given up on life,
or
has life
given up on them?

I don't know who you are or where you are from.
I don't know if you've slept last night, or been
up, tired of fighting this war inside you and
struggling to come to terms with a world that
just won't let you in. I don't know if you are
okay or were crying before this and wanting to
give in to the temptation of ending it all. I
just know that, right now, if you are 'feeling'
something, then you are more alive than a lot of
other people around you, that sensitivity takes
courage, and this world needs courageous souls,
and if your heart seems empty, then maybe it's
just bigger than everybody else's, and has the
capacity to give and take, much, much more.

\#28

She walks
on sunshine
and he
wonders if
summer
is
     here

         to

            stay.

29

I am the warm summer breeze
and the cold winter frost
I am the silence in a gaze
and late midnight talks
I am the words you read
and the lessons you learn
I am the tears you hold
and the joy you serve
I am the dust in the air
and the sunlight falling on it
I am the music of the rain
and the song on your lips
I am the weakest thread
and the strongest rope
I am the swirling feather
and the standing stone
I am space and matter
blood, bones and skin
I am bits of the universe
and I hold a universe within.

30

If you looked through people
and glanced under their skin
you would find madness and calm
good deeds and sin
tears within smiles
and smiles within tears
fear within love
and love within fear
peace and chaos
strength and doubts
layers and masks
inside and out
but one thing you'll stumble upon
is for sure
the craving to be understood
more than before
they will hide it and chide it
and push you away
but inside, everyone
is hoping you'll stay.

31

She saw him hiding in a corner
it was a winter's day
she asked him, 'may I sit here?'
but he shuddered
away.

He said:
Don't stand so close to me
don't look me in the eye
the guilt within may repulse you
it's better not to try.
Don't show me any affection
for I may not return
don't touch and soothe my scars
for yours will surely burn.
Don't spoil your flawless beauty
by touching my uncouth spirit
run away while you may
back to the world where you fit.

She said:
My soul is frozen
I need a little warmth
the world is cold and cruel
and there I find no mirth.
My crimes are worse than yours
I have broken many a heart
their shattered pieces stung my own
now it lies torn apart.
I hate being a trophy woman
being kept upon a shelf
will you let me save your soul
so that I may save myself?

And so he stretched out a hand
and took her fingers in his palm
they sat there side by side
her arm within his arm.

I don't know who helped whom
or if they made it till the end
but it's true
you can salvage much of yours
if you find another soul to mend.

32

And as she stepped out,
the clouds came down
to greet her,
to envelope her in a
misty blanket
and carry her away from
the bitterness
and the prejudices
of this world,
off to the land
where dreams came true.

#33

Is it possible
to be broken beyond help
and still have
the capability
to heal someone else?
I wonder if people,
who become a light
for others,
confine all the dark
inside them,
like holding
an angel and a demon
within
and watching each
take its turn.

\#34

While
they all
fall in love
with
her smile
she waits for
one
who will
fall in love
with
her scars.

#35

She talks of sweet sunrises
but yearns the quiet of sunsets
she dreams of saving the world
but fails to begin with herself
her rehearsed smiles come up
faster than her eyes can match
and like water between her fingers
promises slip through her lips.

#36

And you assume you know her
when all that you were shown
was this blanket of a skin
which covers her fragile bones,
you have not gazed within her heart
or waited patiently for her mind
to give you a slight glimpse
into the world which grows inside,
you have not sensed the
unsteady rhythm of her pulse
anytime she stumbles upon
something she loves,
neither watched the light
in her eyes grow dim
and see her veins darken
with the sorrow that swims,
nor have you heard the melodies
that burst forth from her core
when she finds a day worth living
and her spirit soars,
and you certainly have not felt
the nail imprints inside her palm
every time she barely manages
to control her inner storm.

37

So attuned am I
to this masquerade dress
that my own inner self
seems to be someone else,
and I meet her like
I would meet a stranger
an uncomfortable glance
aware of the danger,
of seeing an acquaintance
from an era long gone
having faded memories
of the time spent along,
thus I better walk away
before it makes my cover blow
for she knows me too well
and what I buried long ago.

She keeps her heart in a box
that has a one way road
she pours in her feelings
and purges all her loads,
she has a keen eye
and sees a little more
the sighs behind their smiles
the tears behind their doors,
she picks up their burdens
and puts them in the box
some have sharpened pieces
and some are jagged rocks,
these pinch and tear her heart
but she's too busy saving theirs
the pain begins to rise
yet she tries not to care,
one day she stops and cries
feeling helpless for the world
they watch her in confusion
as she lies bowed and curled,
then she pulls out the box
and shows them her wounded heart
they turn away disgusted
noticing all the broken parts,
and so she suffers in silence
for her voice was never heard
and they label her 'too sensitive'
like it is a bad word.

39

Do not give me your polished
perfection, this untarnished
glass facade, for all I can
see is a reflection of me and
my glaring imperfections. Give
me yourself, all pain, scars
and bruises, and let's waste
our days in imperfect bliss,
matching yours to mine, finding
some broken pieces that fit and
wiping the dust off those
untouched dreams. And maybe one
day when I find my image gazing
back at me, we can laugh at the
flaws together, wondering which
were yours and which were mine
and how some were simply
meant to stay.

#40

Maybe thunder was lightning's lover
calling out to her as she playfully
darted away from him in the dark.
She would peek out at random
stunning him speechless with her beauty
and by the time he said her name
she would hide in the grey again.
But she was not made for tender love
neither for settling down.
She was fiery, intoxicating, and
blinding, eccentric and electric, she
could brighten his world and destroy it
in a mere matter of seconds.
She could not be tamed.

#41

Give me your
tired bones
and I will
build them a bed
in my arms.
Give me your
broken heart
and I will
spend my life
sewing up its pieces.
Give me your
weakened spirit
and I will
hold your hand
as you learn to walk again.

42

There was a rock inside her chest and it
grew heavier everyday. She tried to lift it
out, but the world kept pushing it back in,
trying to convince her that it was a part
of her and that she herself was stone; rigid,
plain, featureless, waiting to be chiselled
in whichever form they so desired. Yet she
had heard the music of the streams and
bathed in the spray. Gushing, shimmering,
overflowing, it teased her and she slowly
felt herself turn lighter. She realized that
the river was gradually cutting through the
rock, and soon boundless infinitesimal
pieces of her became a part of the water and
it took her away. You can still hear her
voice in the chorus of the cascades and
watch her dance with the rhythm of the rapids.
Her laughter resounds through nature.
She is herself now, and no longer holds to
any definition but her own. You may find her
swirling in the wilderness, seeking other
rocks to free.

Do not pity them
their tears
for they still have
the strength to weep.
Pity the soulless,
the frozen,
the ones who have
 forgotten
what it is like to cry.

She wasted so many days
trying to run away into
the void, hating this world
and all that humanity had
to offer. Most days when she
woke up and looked into
the mirror, all she could
see were two dead ends.
Some mornings she didn't
want to wake up at all.

And then what happened?

The voices in her head
told her a tale and she
grabbed a pen and re-wrote
her story. She became
her own fairy godmother
and knight in shining armor
and began to live in a place
where hurts could heal and
night welcomed day. She
started to love herself and
was her own prince charming.
She kissed herself awake.

\#45

And in the end
we are all going to be
 stories
etched in the sands of time
some will stay
and some will slip away
to create shores
for new ones.

#46

These hands were made for healing,
my love. They do not know the path
towards comfort, of finding warmth in
someone else's grip, of being kissed
and protected as a delicate feather.
They know not of being held. Do not
get me wrong, they do crave solace,
they yearn to rest on your palm, but
do not squeeze them, do not grasp
them too tightly, just stay. Mildly
caress the fingertips if you may. Do
not mistake them when they run to
hold a pen more often than they come
to hold your fingers, and fondly
stroke paper rather than the contours
of your wrist. They have breathed
this way, it is the only way they
know of, and something which is
ingrained from years of loneliness,
cannot be unlearnt
so soon.

47

The moth flutters
towards the flame
but as she approaches,
the shadow of her
wings rises on the
wall, and suddenly
she is reminded of
the immense aspirations
they carry, and so
it is, that she flies
back and forth
torn between the choice
of either making her
dreams immortal, or,
succumbing herself, to
the immortality of love.

Do not
give me love.
Give me
patience,
understanding,
laughter,
and I will
find it there.
Stories
are not made
of heartbeats
but of moments
when
it skips them.

She
began
to feel
wings
where
once she
could only
trace a
cage.

'Hi' I say because I have
nothing else to speak. No one
hears my voice and I don't
listen to them either, unless
they talk of space, or stardust,
or the soul. Sometimes I feel
like we're all just fools
trying to make some sort of
difference in this world,
pretending to be these angels,
with a pack of demons lurking
within. Maybe I'm just being
selfish and trying to save myself
in the guise of saving someone
else. Maybe the ink you read is
all the black blood that has come
leaking out from a *black* heart.

I do not know how deeply
embedded the seeds of
misery are. I do not know
how far down the staunch
roots go, holding to cold
places where the warmth
never reaches. You try to
bring the sun in and burn
them out, but sometimes
sadness has its own flowers
and they have learnt to
blossom in the light.

I feel too much.
I have a tendency
of diving into
other people's
bones and tasting
their sorrows,
trying to figure
out if it is a flavour
I remember or
something yet to be
experienced. I don't
know if you've felt
the same, but
once you've drowned
in sadness only to
savour the sweetness
of survival, it becomes
an addiction. To
jump in every time,
any time,
with anyone,
and wonder if you
will make it to
the surface once again.

53

Some days
I want to be lost.
Some days
I want to be found.
And most days
I exhaust myself
figuring out which one
of the days it is.

#54

Do not define her
by something as
shallow as her looks.
Define her by her heart
her compassion
her strength
her fire
and above all else
the thorns she treads
upon so very gracefully.

In order to
save myself
I must
destroy first
the me
I was told
to be.

You will never catch her because she was never meant to be caught. She's got wings that turn to flames if kept locked too long. They will burn the cage down. Her heart is an ocean with a thousand shipwrecks, but on a vivid blue morning you can still see a tiny boat with a fluttering rainbow sail making its way through.

Do not quit
just yet
Darling.
 Hang on
to these tiny
shreds
of faith.
They will take
you home,
I promise.

So many
spend years
searching
for
soul mates
and yet
forget first
to meet
their own
soul.

She looks in the
mirror
watching shades of
different people
appear in her eyes
and she wonders
if the storytellers
got it all wrong.

Maybe beauty and
the beast are
the same person.

#60

We keep dragging
along that
which has died
within us
and then wonder
why this soul
feels so
 heavy
sometimes.

#61

Those few seconds, between sleep
and wakefulness, between dream
and reality, when you are not
quite sure of where you are,
but, you are so damn certain
of where your heart wants to be.

62

Don't draw me. I've got
too many rough edges.
I'd tear the paper to bits.
Don't paint. I wasn't made
to fit on a canvas, the
brown of my eyes always
overspills. I'll be the broken
nib of your pencil, or the
ink splotches on your hands.
I'll be the messy colour
palette, mixed and matched.
Find traces of me wherever
you go.

He hides too much inside
him behind curtained windows
and padlocked doors,
airtight spaces slowly
filling up with all that he
is afraid to show. Curiosity
gets the better of her some
days, but she learns to be
patient, to wait for it to
brim over, to find some
unseen crevices which may
give way, and he will find
her standing there, catching
all the broken pieces.

Hands stretched in
anticipation,
I wait for the
downpour
of all that I have
denied
myself to feel.

And maybe our dreams
don't come to us
in the way we fancy.
Maybe they take on
this subtle cloak
and sit around a little
hoping that we'll have
the tiniest bit of
courage to step out
and lift the veil.

If I am lost, find me
but do not ask me to
come back just yet.
Sit with me in this
lost place and maybe
you will understand
why I come here too
often, what draws me
to my neverland. Find
me, but bring me back
when I am ready. Maybe
you will get to know
me a little better.
Maybe we can get lost
together.

67

There is blood on my hands
of all the feelings I killed,
of infant attractions choked
before they could breathe.
There is smoke on my lips
for every affection declared
that I rolled within a piece
of paper and watched it burn
between my teeth.

What can I say
I was always scared to love.

#68

I take in
a deep breath
and where
there should be
air filling up
the space
within my ribs,
there is you.

My arms are thin, weak.
But I promise they will
share your burdens.
I will not let you fall.

She had scars in places
that had long lost the
ability to feel and no
one could heal them for
they had gone beyond
saving. But one day she
found him drawing flowers
on the dead fragments
and she scoffed bitterly
for she could not even
sense his touch. And yet
her eyes could see. From
the marks sprouted branches.
And where there had been
death there was now growth.
Slowly but surely she found
her pieces transforming
into hopeful, colourful
visions rather than the
reminders of the pain that
had once left them behind.

#71

And sometimes
in the gaps
 between
heart beats
in the space
 between
seconds
in the silence
 between
these words,
I find *you*.

72

You say that
you are stuck
but you have
come so far from
where you were.
You look behind
yourself and
all you see are
shadows. I look
at you and all
I see is light.

#73

She is homesick
for a home that
does not exist,
lovesick for a
love that never
broke the confines
of her head. But
mostly she is sick
of wanting to
leave every time,
to run away from
every place,
every embrace.

Let me heal darling.
Can't you see I'm sitting
in the dark trying to
stitch myself up? I know
these wounds will scare
you, I can't shatter your
oblivion. You must live
like the world has no
sorrow and I must live
like it is full of it and
search for it at every
turn. So that the moment
it comes and finds us, I
will know how to save you.

75

I have watched you fold
yourself into the invisible
when you thought you
weren't needed. Sticking
to the shadows when the
light seemed too bright,
too clear, like it would pass
right through and show
everything you did not
deem worthy enough.
I have watched you, and
it hurts me every time when
you try to quell your own
glow. For your glow reaches
places you do not know.
For it has reached the dark
within me too.

She is broken
and in the process
of sewing herself up,
she tied knots around
her heart, one time
too many, and though
you may try to untangle
her now and then,
but she is just afraid
of falling apart again.

And I wonder what
pieces you let in
and what you keep
out, what keeps you
awake at night, and
what you hold close
as a lullaby. Some
stories are at the
tip of your tongue
but you still roll
them in, too scared
of the vulnerability,
of emotions too raw
to be shown. You
clamp them in the
centre of your fists,
crushing the flower
and permitting the
thorns to dig in.
Let it out.

78

Poets are sad people.
I think it is one of the
saddest things in the
world to not be able to
find a home anywhere
else apart from these
fragile pieces of paper;
to never find a sense of
belonging outside this
ink. When all the other
places and people seem
so alien yet their pain
is so eerily familiar.
How is this not sad?
And then I wonder about
those who do not find
solace even there, who do
not, cannot, find a refuge
anywhere and live their
lives in desolation. And
thus, maybe it is I who is
blessed even in misery.
Maybe I got lucky.

79

I am beginning to read you
the way one tries to learn
a foreign language. Memorizing
the meaning behind every
gesture, the intent behind
every glance. But I wonder if
I will ever be able to mimic
your grace or the gentle dance
of your fingertips, too fluid
to grasp. My hands have always
been clumsy, letting slip more
than they hold on to. But I am
hoping they hold on to you.

Tell me I am more than
this. That I am more
than the doubts, that
like vines, tighten
around my feet, holding
them hostage and slowly
crawl up my body. That
I am more than the smile
I sometimes cannot feel
touching my own eyes.
Some days I fall asleep
to the sound of the ocean,
waves crashing against my
ears, almost drowning my
heart. Tell me that I am
more than these turbulent
waters. That you will help
me find the way to the
calm seas within.

I have a habit of
filling into empty
spaces. I see too many
crevices in people
that stand vacant and
I tend to piece myself
or mould into whatever
form would fit in
best. The hollow in
their eyes easily
catches mine, maybe
because I know too well
the taste of nothing.

I'm scared that
if you kiss my
neck the feeling
may travel down
to my bones and
my spine might end
up growing wings.

#83

Find me in the silence
in the gaps between the stars
in the seconds just before sunrise.
I am the pause before the climax
the dark before the light
the bare before the beautiful
the last quiet sustaining breath before
the moment that takes your breath away.

84

I do not have any special talents
or abilities. I cannot fly or
perform magic. I cannot sing like
the nightingale or swirl like the
hurricane. Most days, the clouds
within me come forward and obstruct
the sun. Some days, day never comes
and the lone evening sky shows its
fading face, here and there. I only
know the art of observation. I only
know how to listen and watch, and
drink it all in, seeking thirstily
for the very last sips of joy and
sorrow in this world. My wandering
soul is all that I have. Some days,
it feels weak, helpless and frail
in the darkness,
 but most days
 it is enough.

85

I try to write of you
but I can feel my fingers twist
just the way your tongue would
if you had to speak of something
that resides too close to your
heart, too pure to utter it out
in fear that words will ruin all
that which it has built inside
of you. Your eyes are the windows
to your soul, but I was never
good at describing windows.
I always get too mesmerized by
what they show, always end up
staring too long, forgetting what
it is that I was supposed to do.

86

Sometimes people who are broken
are these misfit ill-arranged
structures formed from using
their own pieces too often to
support someone else and helping
others offload their burdensome
pieces into themselves. You only
get better and find solace when
you embrace all the spaces within
and carve your own fragments to
fill some of the gaps. And they
don't always have to perfectly fit.
I have a thousand displaced bits
in my jigsaw but what's the point
of having only one picture to show,
only one story to tell?

87

If I am sinking
without wanting to ever
come up again
pull me up,
but don't pull me out.
Stay with me patiently
as I learn to swim.
Hold me when I crave
to slip back under.
Teach me that it is okay
to visit the depths
as long as I remember
the beauty that lies above.

#88

I think you feel
too much because
your heart is too
big to be held
inside your chest
and there is very
little space between
it and your skin,
so all that touches
you outside,
touches you in.

Leave if you must,
but take
a piece of me
with you.
And if you ever
feel lonely
in any part of
the world,
know that I am here,
by your side.

Every night she sleeps
with the hope
that the morning will
bring out a better person
and the darkness
that engulfs her today,
she will have pushed it away.
And she will be able to
look at the Sun with
the same loving gaze that
she reserves for the stars,
and somehow she will find
refuge in daylight too
or maybe
she will not need refuge at all.

91

There are parts of me
that do not make sense,
quirks that I never
quite found the meaning
of. And then I wonder
maybe these oddities were
not mine to understand.
Maybe they are yours that
you left inside me long
ago so you could find me
again. Maybe every misstep
I took has always been
a step
towards you.

Forgive me, ladies and gentlemen
for a desk and four walls
just don't seem to keep me in.
I keep slipping out through
the window panes,
the cracks and the keyholes,
I keep lifting my head to the stars
when you ask me to follow
the road ahead.
Forgive me for I forget your names
but I have a strange tendency
of remembering your eyes.
I think you hold too much in them.
It shows sometimes.

Author's Note

The Dreamer was created on 18th Sept 2014 as a place where I could pen down and try to make sense of all the random wanderings that went through my restless mind. Gradually, it became a place where I could find others who felt the same way, and I feel blessed to touch so many kindred souls every single day. Thank you for being a part of this amazing journey, your love and enthusiasm for my words is forever a source of motivation to me. To be a dreamer, I believe, is to have faith in the power of our dreams, and the courage and persistence to look beyond all that we see.

Acknowledgment

This book would not have been possible without the constant help and encouragement from several people.

Thanks-

To Ma, Pa, for building me into the strong woman I am; to my sister, for introducing me to the magical world of books; to Aru and Soni, for believing, and for giving me sensible, worldly advice; to Rakshit, for not freaking out at what goes on in my head, being my number one proofreader, and pushing me to let the light in when all I wanted to do was close the window shades and sleep; and lastly, to the girl in the mirror, for not giving up on me- Hey you, we made it.

About The Author

Nihar Sharma is an engineer turned freelance writer and poet, and her poetry blog written under her alias 'The Dreamer' has followers from across the globe. She is a native of Jammu, India, and currently resides in Kansas, US. When she's not writing, she's most likely reading, daydreaming or shooing off the squirrel from her bird feeder.

You can read more of her work at –
Facebook: Facebook.com/thedreamerdiary
Instagram: @thedream_diary
Twitter: @thedream_diary

Lightning Source UK Ltd.
Milton Keynes UK
UKHW012155200820
368567UK00004B/1326